SMALL CLOUD RISING

HOW CREATIVES, DREAMERS, POETS AND MISFITS ARE AWAKENING THE ANCIENT FUTURE CHURCH

DAVE GIBBONS

with ROB WILKINS

Small Cloud Rising

Dave Gibbons with Rob Wilkins

Copyright © 2015 by Dave Gibbons

This title is also available as an ebook at *www.smallcloudrising.com/resources.*

For permission requests, write to the publisher, addressed "Attention: Dave Gibbons" at the address below.

XEALOTS
18842 Teller Ave.
Irvine, CA 92612

www.xealots.org

Design and Illustrations by:
SOLIDUM, The Cause Collective.

www.solidum.cc

Printed in the United States of America
Library of Congress Control Number: 2015935685

First Edition: ISBN # 978-0-9861983-0-4

15 16 17 18 19 20 21 22 / 10 9 8 7 6 5 4 3 2

www.smallcloudrising.com

CONTENTS

Empty your mind...

You put water into a cup,
it becomes the cup.

You put water into the bottle,
it becomes the bottle.

You put it into a teapot,
and it becomes a teapot.

The water can flow.

The water can crash.

Be water, my friend.

— Bruce Lee

ACKNOWLEDGMENTS

Whew! I've rewritten this book probably around 20 times. I've concluded that this book will never quite be finished, as you and others will continue to add deeper reflections and insights via our website. I really do see this as a book in progress. I got help from the master, Rob Wilkins, who helped me synthesize this monumental work. Thanks for your joy and patience, Rob! I also received a ton of advice, editorial comments, and feedback from a group of friends like Jacqueline Quan, John Ing, Daniel Ross, Sam Song, Patricia DeWit, Dave Brubaker, Peichi Waite, my wife Rebecca and a whole crew of others. They have patiently waited more than five years as we carefully edited this book down from hundreds of pages to these few.

With this book, my dream is that my friends who are the misfits, the outsiders, the fringe, and sometimes the jaded, the cynical, and those tired of religion and insular institutionalism are loved and celebrated. Your life in the margins has given you a vision of what is ahead! You're the new wineskin, still respectful of the ancient purposes of the church. You've been entrusted with forming this cloud, but with a Spirit of love and joy, partnering with the many different types of churches and communities God is growing. We'll know we're healthy when church isn't Bridezilla to us anymore, but this beautiful bride God has given us to love and cherish.

My hope is that beyond professional pastors, many would see they are all part of this new cloud rising. This new cloud is a group of misfits, dreamers, wild ones, poets, innovators, entrepreneurs, creatives, artists, young, old, quiet, loud, crazy, diverse...a global crew rising, being the church wherever they go. This storm of saints cannot be contained by land or boxes.

CLOUDS:
FREED TO ROAM
AND BLESS

It is better to have your head in the clouds, and know where you are than to breathe the clearer atmosphere below them, and think that you are in paradise.

— Henry David Thoreau

CHAPTER 1
BUILDING BABEL

1.

In the days following the terrible flood, Noah's ancestors shared one language, a common color of skin, and a great dream.

Settling on a plain, they looked to the sky and someone imagined building through the clouds.

Genesis 11:3-9 tells the story:

> *They said to each other, "Come, let's make bricks and bake them thoroughly." They used brick instead of stone, and tar for mortar.*
>
> *Then they said, "Come, let us build ourselves a city, with a tower that reaches to the heavens, so that we may make a name for ourselves; otherwise*

we will be scattered over the face of the whole earth."

But the Lord came down to see the city and the tower the people were building. The Lord said, "If as one people speaking the same language they have begun to do this, then nothing they plan to do will be impossible for them. Come, let us go down and confuse their language so they will not understand each other."

So the Lord scattered them from there over all the earth, and they stopped building the city. That is why it was called Babel — because there the Lord confused the language of the whole world. From there the Lord scattered them over the face of the whole earth.

•

Heat rose in waves above the earth's dusty ground.

For three years and counting, no rain fell.

Death loomed.

Crops wasted.

Hope evaporated.

Will the drought never end?

Unexpectedly, a hunted prophet risked meeting a powerful king. The people knew him as Elijah, and called him The Voice.

1 Kings 18:41-44 picks up the story:

> *Elijah said to Ahab, "Up on your feet! Eat and drink — celebrate! Rain is on the way; I hear it coming."*

> *Ahab did it: got up and ate and drank. Meanwhile, Elijah climbed to the top of Carmel, bowed deeply in prayer, his face between his knees. Then he said to his young servant, "On your feet now! Look toward the sea."*

> *He went, looked, and reported back, "I don't see a thing."*

> *"Keep looking," said Elijah, "seven times if necessary."*

And sure enough, the seventh time he said, "Oh yes, a cloud! But very small, no bigger than someone's hand, rising out of the sea."

In each of these Old Testament narratives, the clouds captivate me. It began to occur to me as a metaphor for the church.

As a pastor high on a tower looking down and as a servant leader searching all around, I have seen clouds from both sides.

Your perspective as you move through the clouds makes all the difference in the world:

Up for recognition or down in blessing.

2.

I still remember police lights bouncing off the windshield of my dad's car, and my crying mother huddled in the back seat with a knife in her hand.

As a child of 11, a surreal dream began in my head: It was a film of my mom's undoing in a spiral of alcoholism, eating disorders, bleeding ulcers, and a never-healing heart.

Talked out of the car by her pastor, my mother walked past me, sobbing so hard she could barely stand, and said:

Your father had an affair.

With one swift cut, my mother lost her savior on more levels than one.

As an American military man in South Korea, my father had swept her away from her impoverished and war-scarred land to pursue the American dream.

In a strobe of colors and sirens, she wept so hard she could hardly breathe.

3.

In 1994, I started Newsong in the multiethnic city of Irvine, California, for people like my mom. Her legacy shaped the vision of our church.

Possessing her Korean genes, I knew what it felt like to be an outcast in America.

A stranger in a foreign land, I understood the depth of her isolation.

Owning her pain, I learned dreams could never be made of money.

Feeling her betrayal, I vowed that Newsong would be a place for an outcast like her, as well as all other misfits.

A place to find the living water Jesus promised.

4.

When Jesus spoke to the woman at the well, he was addressing a woman like my mom.

Not the right ethnicity. Not a man. Not a pure woman, by any means.

The woman, exiled to visit the well alone, engaged in a culturally-barred conversation with a man from a foreign land.

Instead of judging her, Jesus offered this outcast living water.

John 4 picks up the thread:

Woman:

> *Sir, you don't even have a bucket to draw with, and this well is deep. So how are you going to get this living water? Are you a better man than our ancestor Jacob, who dug this well and drank from it, he and his sons and livestock, and passed it down to us?*

Jesus:

> *Everyone who drinks this water will get thirsty again and again. Anyone who drinks the water I give will never thirst—not ever. The water I give will be an artesian spring within, gushing fountains of endless life.*

5.

Years following her betrayal, I remember rushing outside after hearing my mother crying late one night.

When I held her emaciated, alcoholic, ulcerated body, I had no words to ease her pain. I would just hold her shaking body. I didn't know what else to do.

6.

Until she was killed in a hit-and-run on Arizona I-10 in 1981, my mom could find no relief from her spiraling pain.

Despite good intentions, our family's church didn't know how to walk with my mom.

She remained the awkward immigrant, struggling with the language, culturally different, isolated in pain.

HAPPIEST PLACE ON EARTH???

7.

Shortly after Newsong was named one of the fastest growing churches in America, I sensed a disillusionment about our church seeping in while we were next to Mickey Mouse's house.

For our Easter Experience in 2005, we chose Anaheim Convention Center, which is so close to Disneyland, I could have thrown a rock and hit Sleeping Beauty's castle.

The event would have made Walt proud.

The Magic Kingdom and The Holy Spirit.

Collectively, we wished upon a star, and thousands of people streamed in, guided by parking attendants wearing large white Mickey Mouse gloves.

Festive banners flew.

Digital screens and colorful spotlights lit up the place.

The Gospel choir rocked.

Dancers stretched for the sky.

Beats of bass blasted.

The energy in the place shot through the clouds.

Taking a peek from behind the curtain at the massive crowd, I heard an unexpected, still voice.

I believe God spoke a question to me:

IS THIS IT?

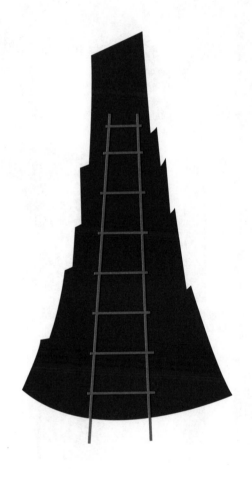

8.

The Tower of Babel moves up through the clouds for glory.

The building of Babel exhibits the motivation of the human heart to promote oneself against the welfare of others. In our desire to make a name for ourselves, we are more than content to rise on the backs of others.

Vertical builds are in our nature. Before we know it, we are caught up in a race to build the tallest towers — skyscraping, humongous containers of our best ideas and selves.

To separate ourselves from others.

To rise above the clouds.

Shortly after my return from Bangkok, I began to wonder: *Is Newsong just another kind of Babel?*

Following the success of an outreach that drew nearly 5,000 people, I could only envision one formula for continuing that kind of momentum:

A series of capital campaigns to build more walls.

As the ongoing efforts sucked our church's time, attention, and resources, I continually reminded people:

It's not about the building. It's about what happens inside the building.

With a strong vision for building bigger, I slowly began to see the walls were killing us.

From the church's inability to reach outcasts like my mother, I learned these lessons about walls:

They isolate, separate, and eventually turn into mirrors.

When people talked about church, they meant the building.

Instead of following a mysterious movement of the Spirit, the church became a fixed location.

You could plug it into your GPS.

Stripped from our community and culture, we begin to look and act the same.

We created the same jargon, art, music, and programs that attracted others like ourselves.

WHAT
WOULD
THE CHURCH
LOOK LIKE
IF IT
WASN'T
CONTAINED
ON A PIECE
OF LAND?

Having started out with the desire to reach misfits, we ended up back in Babel with a devotion to the same kind of tame — a bland conformity to a misdirected dream.

At the pinnacle of success, parallel to Disneyland, God asked me to look deeply into my motivations, metrics, and methods.

I had created a box, my own Babel, a kingdom with walls. We knew how to manufacture experiences and draw in thousands of spectators, but failed to impact our city by any meaningful measure.

We grew vertically.

The city did not change.

The power of big was contained in a box.

I felt God ask me,

> *What would the church look like if it wasn't contained on a piece of land?*

I had no idea.

9.

The metaphor of clouds may have first risen in my mind through the persistent love of Susie Lee, an early investor in Newsong.

Susie had left our church to serve in Bangkok. That is where I visited after Newsong had been outbid for a prime piece of land near a major California interstate.

> *By the brothers and sisters of my own ethnic heritage,* I told Susie. *A Korean car company let it be known they would bid slightly more than whatever the church offered.*

I told her I thought God might be calling me out of my role as pastor.

Sensing my deep funk, she insisted I come to Bangkok to plant a church.

I laughed, because I thought it was a pretty good joke.

In her 60s, with the energy and tenacity of a 20-year-old, she said that she wasn't kidding.

I told her the locals would do a much better job.

She looked me in the eyes and said:

You need to come.

When I promised to send someone else over, she repeated:

YOU need to come.

In my days of hemming and hawing, she repeated the same mantra over and over.

One day, after reading a Scripture stating that the harvest was plentiful and laborers few, I experienced a *Matrix-*like download, where all the digits cascaded and secrets were unlocked, and a voice came to me again.

I believed the voice was God's, saying the same thing as Susie, but with a little greater urgency:

Go Now.

With Susie's persistent and gentle love, a small cloud formed with the promise of rain in the desert of my heart.

She saw it rise before I could.

Our birth is but a sleep and a forgetting.
Not in entire forgetfulness,
and not in utter nakedness,
but trailing clouds of glory do we come.

— William Wordsworth

CHAPTER 2
ONE

1.

A few months later, I was granted a sabbatical from Newsong and my whole family was living in Bangkok in Apartment 24N.

In my mind, the N came to stand for Narnia. This would be a year more wild and exciting than anything we could have imagined.

Inspired by the challenge of bringing the Gospel to Thailand, a country that was less than one percent Christian despite a 100-year presence of Christianity, I immediately ramped up ministry.

Operating in my default mode of bigger equals better, our first outreach service drew unprecedented numbers of people.

Instead of joy, our core people from the start-up seemed dejected.

What's wrong? I asked.

Thailand isn't Newsong, they said.

In Thailand, people walk in their neighborhoods.

They know each other by name.

Instead of spectate, people like to talk with one another.

Instead of isolate, people come together in suffering.

Fast-paced is an American like me, coming to teach them a thing or two.

Slowing down, I learned to listen and heard them say:

I want to be known.

That's when it hit me. That's different than making a name for yourself.

2.

While rediscovering this centrality of relationship, Boyd was another small cloud rising for me.

During a test service held in a bar in the Sukhumvit district of Bangkok, Boyd listened intently to the message.

A young, ordinary-looking man, he approached me in a humble manner.

With great passion, Boyd explained:

I am new in faith to Christ.

I loved the service.

Out of the blue, Boyd asked me:

Would you disciple me?

Turns out, Boyd was one of Thailand's most famous singers.

He possessed an 80-percent personal brand recognition

in a country of 65 million.

Boyd and I became good friends. I advised him on business-related matters, his dreams, and spiritual life.

He helped reverse my metrics for church success.

I led Newsong believing influence was measured by bigger numbers. I could easily envision 30,000 people at multiple campuses globally.

Boyd showed me a different way to calculate.

He was just one person, but known by more than 50 million people.

That's when it hit me:

It's not about the mass; it's about the one.

Love occurs at the speed of one relationship at a time.

3.

Boyd taught me that influence moves from the fringes.

A rock star living in the light of the Good News.

The Bible started to come alive with examples:

>   An Ethiopian eunuch.

>   A mass-murdering Jew.

>   A whore with perfume.

>   A carpenter from Nazareth.

In God's scheme of things, a prostitute by the name of Rahab ends up holding the keys to the city.

4.

In Thailand, undistracted by gadgets and pressing deadlines, I could hear:

The sound of laughter.

The pain of one suffering.

The rage or sigh of an outcast.

The hope in a praise song.

The persistence in prayer.

They all spoke the same thing to me:

My vision for Newsong was wrong.

5.

After Elijah's servant saw the small cloud rising, a storm quickly rose on the horizon.

1 Kings tells us:

> *The sky grew black with wind-driven clouds, and then a huge cloudburst of rain, with Ahab hightailing it in his chariot for Jezreel.*

And then, all of a sudden, there's Elijah, hiking up his robe, running in front of the king's chariot, leading the way.

Upon my return to Newsong, rethinking church through the metaphor of the cloud, I could begin to imagine the smile on the old prophet's leathery face.

6.

Returning home from Bangkok, I apologized to the church:

> *I think I have created something that is not after God's heart.*

All the walls we built were locking us in.

Then I painted a vision of a cloud moving with the wind.

And its promise of blessing.

7.

In Babel, the people's greatest fear is the very thing God desires: To be scattered over the face of the earth.

After creation, God told Adam and Eve:

> *Be fruitful and multiply. Fill the earth and govern it. Reign over the fish in the sea, the birds in the sky, and all the animals that scurry along the ground.*

Again, the metaphor sprung in my mind. Like a cloud, I envisioned the church designed to roam and bless the earth.

I encouraged our people to see ourselves as co-owners of God's world and how every step we take lands us on holy ground.

8.

When the disciples of Jesus showed up, they were shocked to see Jesus talking with a woman at the well.

A loose Samaritan to boot.

Intimidated by the disciples, inspired by Jesus, the woman left her pot at the well, racing off to the village where she had been shamed.

By the time Jesus explained to his disciples the kingdom at hand, the woman was saying:

Come and see.

9.

Bradley Rapier, a USC professor of Hip Hop known for his creative choreography, told me this about the art of dance:

It's about the groove, not the move.

Instinctively, I knew that Newsong had all the moves, but lacked the groove.

Clueless about how to develop a groove, I started with our faulty moves.

We can have a form of religion, the Apostle Paul insisted, but not have the Spirit.

Despite our ability to draw large numbers of people, our church seemed irrelevant and dated.

If it's true that God walks through the city dressed in His people, the church walls blocked our view.

For Newsong, the kingdom at hand was mostly limited to what happened inside the church's walls. Spending most of our resources on growing bigger, we had failed to engage our culture and love our neighbors. Like Babel, we were growing up and not out.

As if I needed any further evidence, my own children weren't buying it. Along with many other young people, they had checked out of church.

My second daughter experienced the best in terms of leaders, programs, and activities, but still found church boring compared to what her peers offered through parties, alcohol, and drugs.

She was made for the wild. What we were offering was artificial, formulaic, and orderly. The way we were engaging and equipping her was antiquated.

The mystery and danger of God seemed lost in the way we were doing church. I knew something deep had to change.

It wasn't just about a new curriculum or youth pastor. We had to fundamentally adjust how we engaged with beliefs, values, the marginalized, programs, resource development, outsiders, collaboration, innovation, cross-cultural divides, misfits, music, and more.

I had this strange feeling of needing to turn things upside down.

Instead of rising up through the clouds, I imagined a church descending like rain in blessing.

The air moves like a river
and carries the clouds with it;
just as running water carries
all the things that float upon it.

— Leonardo da Vinci

CHAPTER 3
FLOW

1.

Clouds flow.

As I began to grapple with how to reshape Newsong, the imagery of clouds captivated my imagination.

Like a kid on his back on a windy, summer day, I was enthralled.

2.

In seeking to become a church without walls, this was the first thing on my agenda:

Get rid of my agenda.

I gladly discarded an endless series of capital campaigns to build more walls.

I had surrounded myself with our best people to achieve my vision. The suck of human and financial resources required for the ongoing building of more walls diseased our church.

Instead of rallying people around the pastor's dream, I wondered:

> *What if we equipped our people to discover — and live — each person's God-given destiny?*

Radical shifts were required. Instead of spending 70 percent of my own time on sermon preparation, I would shift that figure to human development.

Other paradoxical shifts in vision occurred:

> Small is big.
>
> Pain can be transformed into positive power.
>
> Reach the fringes for maximum impact.
>
> Neighbor means someone who's not just like you.
>
> Preaching to people isn't as important as loving them.

Instead of inviting people into the church with the hope of building Babel together, we began to brainstorm how we could help them flow out into the world in blessing.

3.

Shortly after my return, an 86-year-old woman tightly grasped my hand.

> *The secret for the church's revival is Trinitarian unity,* she insisted.

In God, each of the three persons lives in seamless rhythms of self-giving and serving, the glory going to the other.

And round and round, in His great love, God goes, spilling out into all of creation.

Jesus prayed in John 17:

> *I pray that they will all be one, just as you and I are one — as you are in me, Father, and I am in you. And may they be in us so that the world will believe you sent me. I have given them the glory you gave me, so they may be one as we are one. I am in*

them and you are in me. May they experience such perfect unity that the world will know that you sent me and that you love them as much as you love me. Father, I want these whom you have given me to be with me where I am. Then they can see all the glory you gave me because you loved me even before the world began!

Joy is the name of the woman who opened my eyes to this transformative flow.

In her bright eyes, you could see she saw the cloud.

4.

Around the concept of flow, we began to imagine a new way of equipping our people.

Flow was about helping each person:

Discover who God made him or her to be.

Strip away false-prophet lies about identity.

Live through their unique gifting, personality, and experiences.

See, know, affirm, and bless others.

Develop all of the above in loving community.

5.

In a ceaseless cycle, water flows through all three states of being: liquid, vapor, and solid.

Blessings happen through endless transformations.

6.

When the woman at the well asked for living water, Jesus revealed intimate details of her life.

He knew her, but not in a way like any other.

Many knew her physically.

Many called her a half-breed.

Many considered her an inferior creature.

Jesus saw her as a beloved child of God.

7.

Frederick Buechner writes:

The truth is: we are our names. That simple. Biblical people knew this without any explanation. A name was presence. So when they talk about the name of God, they are talking about the presence of God. Name-presence. Presence-name. Same thing. Like in our collects. We pray in the Name of Jesus Christ — in other words, in Jesus' presence — right here and now.

A church is a collection of names of people with unique and supernatural identities.

8.

In Babel, just one name is mentioned.

Let us make a name for ourselves.

The effort to build more walls required a one-size-fits-all training manual focused on unleashing the power of the mass.

Names are not really necessary for achieving the success of someone else's dream.

In a nameless culture, everyone began to:

Look the same.

Do the same.

Require the same.

Conform to the norm.

It was all the same kind of same in a place without names.

As I pondered Newsong's future, I knew the first step was to know one another's name.

9.

In the story, the woman at the well remains nameless.

I believe John, a master writer, intentionally chose to do so.

Anonymously, she represents:

> Every person thirsting to be known.

> Nameless people from the fringe.

The woman at the well appeared to Jesus, alone, exiled as a moral outcast, a person judged to be of inferior gender, race, religion, and value.

When the disciples saw Jesus talking to her, they muttered among themselves about the scandal of such a thing.

Leaving her water pot at the well, the woman raced off into the village proclaiming:

Come, see a man who told me everything I ever did.

Flowing begins when you are known.

As the disciples pondered their master's dignity, streams of foreigners from the fringe were already flowing toward Jesus.

A cloud is made of billows upon billows
upon billows that look like clouds.
As you come closer to a cloud
you don't get something smooth,
but irregularities at a smaller scale.

— *Benoit Mandelbrot*

CHAPTER 4
FROM THE FRINGE

1.

It took seven times for Elijah's searching servant to see the small cloud rising.

Blessing begins with something nearly invisible.

2.

The great movements in human history almost always
rise from the fringe:

>   A black man from Alabama with a dream.
>   Peasants in the streets of Paris.
>   A man with wild hair who failed math.
>   A carpenter from Nazareth.

As we began to equip people in the process of flowing,
our focus shifted from the masses to those on the fringe:

>   The marginalized.
>   The outcasts.
>   The misfits.
>   The widowed.
>   The entrepreneurs.
>   The orphaned.
>   The aberrant.
>   The outsiders.
>   The freaks.

The creatives.

The poor.

All the people not great at building Babel walls.

Our decision to focus on the fringe was grounded in a good reason:

Jesus did it.

We began to see the power from redeemed suffering.

3.

In her childhood home, at the age of seven, Maribel shattered a mirror.

Staring at her cracked image, she wondered again:

Who am I?

Am I a mistake or a miracle?

The evidence surrounding her seemed contradictory.

Born two months premature to a woman once diagnosed as barren, experiencing endless cycles of abuse and abandonment, Maribel's survival seemed a miracle.

At the same time, there was this:

Whenever Papa molested her, she felt worthless.

Having picked up a mirror shard, Maribel walked into a closet and stabbed herself in the abdomen.

She hoped the life would flow out of her.

4.

The rising walls of Babel are designed to make us feel safe.

Power in numbers.

Protection from danger.

Comfort in us.

Separation from others.

It's like being in the womb of a warm cocoon, safe and tame.

As we moved toward the metaphor of the cloud, Newsong tore down walls built on false-prophet promises of safety, fulfillment, comfort, and eventual influence.

Freed to roam and bless like clouds means taking perilous turns.

At the mercy of the wind, you are bound to run into danger.

As we began to move our people out into the world, equipped to bless, we quickly learned risk paid dividends.

We started to see this:

Sometimes the church gets to be the danger.

It's like the old prophet telling the king that he'd better get on his golden chariot and hightail it out of there before the storm of blessing came.

5.

At the age of 14, Maribel had sex with her friend's dad in exchange for money.

When her mother learned of the incident, she asked Maribel what the name of her lover was.

In great shame, Maribel whispered his name.

> *Good*, her mother replied, *now you have someone who will take care of you.*

6.

Well before the small cloud rose, Elijah was confident a three-year drought was about to end.

In the middle of suffering, he drew his insight from the track record of God's provision.

The food the ravens fed him.

The drinks of a widow when the brook dried up.

The jar of flour continually full.

The jug of oil never dry.

Emerging from the fringes, Elijah boldly called King Ahab to a duel.

Whose God could first consume a sacrifice?

Gathered on a mountain, Elijah was convinced the odds were with him:

450 prophets to one.

He graciously gave them the first shot.

1 Kings picks up the story with Elijah trash-talking:

> *By noon, Elijah had started making fun of them, taunting:*
>
> *Call a little louder — he is a god, after all.*
>
> *Maybe he's off meditating somewhere or other, or maybe he's gotten involved in a project, or maybe he's on vacation.*
>
> *You don't suppose he's overslept, do you, and needs to be woken up?*

I love the mental picture of an old prophet taunting the staggering odds of the powers that be.

As we sought to encourage our people to take risks in the name of Jesus, we taught them that Elijah's confidence was rooted in two realities:

God's provision.

False prophets can't help but tell lies.

7.

Having survived a childhood rife with abuse, prostitution, drug dealing, abandonment, and organized crime, Maribel met a wealthy man of shady intentions.

Moving into a house on a Pacific Ocean cliff, Maribel collected names of prestige — Porsche, Gucci, Cartier — to stitch together a new identity.

Beautiful and expansive were the views from her new home.

A trophy wife, until the pregnancy test ended the dream. Following Maribel's third abortion, her husband abandoned her.

8.

From the fringes come the helpless.

Having suffered, they know the power of pain.

They don't buy the lies of our culture's Red Lipstick Prophets, selling promises of unending beauty, comfort, and personal fulfillment.

Living on the fringe, all false hope quickly evaporates.

If the pain does not first kill or numb them, people on the fringe experience the flow of a supernatural God because they are broken open.

When people from the fringe discover the courage to step out in faith, they often experience a supernatural transformation of their pain into a power to relieve the suffering of others.

Divinely known in brokenness:

> The woman at the well.
>
> Elijah in the drought.
>
> Maribel standing amid broken shards of mirror.

From the fringes, we have discovered places of suffering where God's love freely moves in the flow of blessing. What was meant for destruction is our salvation.

9.

Years later, in a failing marriage with a man who loved her, Maribel's pain surfaced in self-destruction.

Turns out, pain like hers doesn't just go away.

At the same time she was separated from her husband and three children, she was forced to care for her dying mother, who never seemed to care much for her.

Even during moments of rare sobriety, Maribel could no longer see straight.

When her mother found Jesus on her deathbed, Maribel fell into a deep depression. She couldn't stomach the idea that her mother was forgiven for all the wrong she had done to her.

10.

As we began to examine ways to train and equip our people, we realized the power of suffering in shaping a life. It kept us from focusing exclusively on gifts, attributes, and qualities.

In the context of a loving community, we now saw suffering as a critical catalyst in shaping a unique blessing.

We learned that pain:

> Points us to our destiny, where we can serve others based on how we have suffered.

> Gives credibility to our voice.

> Connects us to each other on common human ground.

> Provides a fellowship of suffering that binds us.

> Breaks people open for the flow of living water.

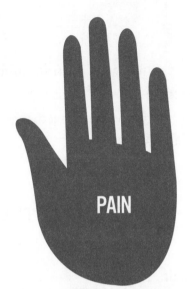

PAIN

JESUS IS
THE ONLY
ONE WITH
SCARS IN
HEAVEN
SCARS
CAN BE
BEAUTIFUL

11.

When a friend invited her to Newsong, Maribel's desperation was greater than her mistrust of church.

If something didn't change, she knew she was going to die.

Even more than stepping inside, Maribel shocked herself by raising her hand before the pastor led prayer for those with burdens.

During the prayer, she experienced the love of Jesus.

> *Jesus met me, embraced me, loved me,* Maribel says. *A new life began inside of me. Each day was filled with wonder and beauty.*

12.

In the heat of the sun, a drop of water evaporates.

Transformed into a new state of being, a tiny vapor rises, designed to collect with others.

HOW DO CLOUDS FORM?

*There are no rules of architecture for
a castle in the clouds.*

— *Gilbert K. Chesterton*

Constant kindness can accomplish much.
As the sun makes ice melt,
kindness causes misunderstanding,
mistrust, and hostility to evaporate.

—— Albert Schweitzer

CHAPTER 5
THE CLOUD

1.

A cloud forms as water vapors condense onto dust particles from strange places — volcanic eruptions, bits of salt released through the crashing of waves, and outer space.

Around abrasion, individual water vapors collect.

2.

Within the walls of Babel, belonging required a singular focus.

We trained our people if we found them useful.

From a standard manual, we equipped people who helped accomplish our vision of rising through the clouds.

More than anything, Babel was an engineering feat.

Human development became about making our people even more useful.

Processes and operations were efficiently synced for a homogenous mass where we all learned the necessary jargon, skills, and prescribed roles to get the job of building more walls done.

Nearly all of our job descriptions engaged projects and programs inside our walls.

We asked an entrepreneur to lead a church Bible study and requested an artist to paint crosses in the nursery.

Most of our resources went to creating spectacle and precious little into shaping lives.

By failing to know and equip our people, one creation at a time, we defrocked them of their priestly roles in the real world.

We began to witness mechanically and call that evangelism.

Because we looked more and more the same, we branded others because unique people scared us.

The walls we built clearly demarcated what was inside and out.

Ill-equipped to engage suffering in the fringe, the best we could do was invite people into our strange and tame little world.

If they liked it there, we promised them equipping tools they could download from our website.

Instead of knowing their names, we asked them to sign up.

In the process, we missed my mom and all the people like her, who thought themselves to be worthless.

3.

Maribel came to Xealots, our nonprofit organization designed to help equip our people, just after we launched. Maribel was just the sort of person we had in mind — a socially-conscious misfit whose life was distorted by suffering.

A few months after her baptism, Maribel attended a Xealots conference at Newsong. Two of the people featured were Benny and Janice Yu, who shared their story of working with victims of human trafficking in Mexico City.

Maribel remembers:

My heart was like — this is God talking to me.

At the same time, she felt deep inadequacy.

All she had were the broken pieces of her life.

And endless questions:

How could God use someone like me?

Where can I find healing?

How can I belong in a transparent, loving community?

Where can I get training?

How do I find out who I really am?

In the middle of her questions, Maribel felt the call of God to go to Mexico City and visit the Yus. She didn't have any idea what she might encounter.

I simply made a leap of faith, Maribel recalls.

4.

Direction is everything.

Babel rises up through the clouds.

In the years previous to my trip to Thailand, I rallied our people around my vision to grow bigger.

I did so by:

> Inspiring the masses.
>
> Measuring progress in steps, stages, and numbers.
>
> Asking people to give to the next capital campaign.

At the same time I kept telling them the sky was the limit, I realized the sky had no limit.

Year after year, with great diligence, effort, and faith, our people labored to rise.

In the communities where our campuses were located, a lot of people came to know the name of Newsong.

They just didn't believe we made any difference.

5.

During her trip to Mexico, Maribel stayed a week with the Yus, who were in the early stages of setting up house and completing paperwork for their ministry.

The Yus introduced Maribel to Valerie, a missionary in the red light district of Mexico City, who invited her to visit some of the girls she helped.

In the ragged community, Maribel experienced powerful moments of unmasked suffering, as well as God's redeeming love at work.

A few days later, Valerie told Maribel she and her fiancé were planning a visit to a small village in Mexico.

Maribel recognized the town's name immediately:

The place where her father still lived.

Valerie asked Maribel if she might want to come along.

6.

As we began to implement customized training, the metaphor of the cloud again seized my imagination.

On a natural level, a cloud yields life-giving water.

On a supernatural level, a cloud yields living water.

Instead of rising up through the clouds for recognition, what if we descended with blessing like rain?

Instead of honing people's skills through technique, what if we developed our people through love?

Instead of exhausting resources to build more walls, what if we invested into our people?

Instead of making a name for ourselves, what if we learned the names of others?

Then it came to me. The cloud is both a HOME and an ACADEMY.

A home because the focus is on love, lived out in meaningful relationships (God and others).

An academy because we equip.

The purpose is to serve those we are called to love. By doing so, our people flourish in all domains of society, rather than simply serving the interests of one pastor or leader to build one vertical institution.

The church is artfully described in Scriptures as a Family, One Body, a Bride, a Flock, a House, an Army, and a City on a Hill. All these are expressions of the church being a HOME and an ACADEMY, where we embody all these things! It's like X-MEN Academy, where we invite mutants into our house of love to equip them to make a difference, not by themselves, but along with others with different superpowers.

What if we truly equipped our people to live beyond the church infrastructure? Then the potential for making a difference becomes exponential.

We become a church, a cloud, no longer limited by geographical or physical boundaries.

7.

In the car ride from Mexico City to her hometown, Maribel shared her story of childhood abuse with Valerie.

After listening, Valerie asked her gently:

Have you forgiven your father because you now see him through God's eyes?

No, Maribel responded.

Truth be told, she couldn't even imagine the possibility.

As they dropped Maribel off at her aunt's house, Valerie prayed for eyes to see in new ways.

After a visit with family, including many aunts and cousins, Maribel's father said he needed to leave to catch a bus to take him home.

Maribel walked her father to the porch and they were alone.

In her head, she heard:

The way he called her a mistake when he molested her.

The echoing prayers of Valerie.

Having learned how love casts out fear, this is what Maribel said:

> *Dad, I forgive you and I love you because Jesus first loves and forgives me.*

When she prayed for him, her father repeated her words.

As Maribel saw her father in a new light, so did Papa for his daughter.

In her father's eyes, for the first time, he saw reflected a treasure, not a mistake.

8.

After her return from Mexico, Maribel was asked to join a group of about 20 Xealots — a mixture of young and seasoned Christians, greatly diverse, all sharing a passion to serve people on the fringes.

In helping train and equip our people, we desired to create a place for people to belong. Much in the same way water vapors collect to form a cloud, we understood the critical nature of coming together as one.

We believed an ongoing cycle of transformation occurs inside a culture of community, and that abrasion provides places for deep connection.

Living life together, open with their pain, our people find freedom to love, learn, and serve in any culture and unleash beauty, even in the midst of discomfort.

He loads the clouds with moisture;
he scatters his lightning through them.
At his direction they swirl around
over the face of the whole earth
to do whatever he commands them.
He brings the clouds to punish people,
or to water his earth and show his love.

—Job 37:11-13

CHAPTER 6

CONDENSATION

1.

Two significant interpretations exist for ecclesia, the Greek word we translate as church.

The word literally means: Called out ones.

Called out of self.

Called out to love God and the other.

Called out to be different and make a difference.

In its early interpretation, the church was called out of the world into an assembly.

With a later emphasis, ecclesia focused on the church

called out to be a blessing.

Both interpretations are correct.

The cloud cycle teaches us about a process of ongoing transformation, a rhythm of moving in and out of assembly and blessing. Turns out, you can't have one without the other.

2.

After sharing a part of her childhood story of abuse, Maribel was prayed over in a community of people who loved her.

In one prayer, she was described as a flower of the sea.

Following the prayer, Maribel told them her name literally meant "star of the sea."

Maribel was in disbelief. Someone knew the meaning of her name. And that name might be true.

3.

Different perspectives are required to understand flow.

Stories are needed to help us see.

After healing a man, Jesus tells the Pharisees he only does what he sees his Father doing.

The explanation is in John 5:

> *For the Father loves the Son and shows him everything he is doing. In fact, the Father will show him how to do even greater works than healing this man. Then you will truly be astonished.*
>
> *For just as the Father gives life to those he raises from the dead, so the Son gives life to anyone he wants.*

Flow is self-giving love, moving from the heart of eternity miraculously out into time.

•

In the movie *Chocolat*, a quiet village exists in the French countryside — a place of authority, regimen, and understood roles.

It is a beautifully bland land, carefully ordered, where no one ever asks for more.

On a winter day, arriving at the same time as a rare north wind, Vianne Rocher, a single mother and chocolatier, opens up shop.

To make the decadence worse, Vianne customizes her creations to each guest's precise taste.

At the same time the people of the town are drawn to experience the exotic, vagabonds arrive from the river, and chaos ensues.

Flow moves unconventionally, almost always against the currents of the traditional.

•

The room erupts with the smell of expensive perfume poured by a prostitute onto the feet of Jesus.

Flow revels in ridiculous extravagance.

4.

In developing our training process called Flow, our desire was to help each person live out his or her destiny.

The process most closely resembles an excavation. It isn't so much about people changing; it's about them being supernaturally unearthed.

A loving community gently excavates, like amazed archaeologists, all that God intended, diligently watching for beauty that has been there all along.

Excavation requires digging God's true identity out from layers of buried life, fear, and sin.

In the context of this community, leaders look at people as treasure maps, and look for Xs that mark the spot.

Instead of a one-size-fits-all approach aimed at the masses, we felt the training needed to be unorthodox, tailored to each person's unique design.

Flow would include experiences, written and unwritten content, mentors, different cultures, and friendships outside their familiar context.

A key part of Flow involves listening to and entering each other's stories in a diverse and loving community.

In a shared story, the names appear and take on life.

5.

In her community, Maribel was drawn to one particular woman.

With Susan, Maribel shared a history of suffering.

> *There was an immediate bond for reasons I could not figure out at first. Eventually, she shared her story and then I knew. Her story was very similar to mine — a mentally ill mother, a childhood of abuse, bickering, and a string of tragic incidents. I knew then why God put us together.*

During a Flow consultation, designed to discern gifts and obstacles in a person's life, Susan stunned Maribel.

After hearing Maribel's story, she looked her friend in the eyes and said:

> *You were made to mother and you will be a mother to many!*

Up until that moment, Maribel never saw herself gifted to mother, even with her own children, much less for others.

I felt like I didn't deserve to have my children. Two of my best friends had lost children, and I couldn't understand why. I was the one who had five abortions, and let people do what they wanted with my body.

It was a transitional moment for Maribel.

For her to see that gift, which was so buried to me. It broke my heart and gave me hope at the same time. I was a mom because of God's grace, the way He created me, and the children He gave me.

When she said, "You are a Mom," I said, "Yes!"

At the same time Maribel found a direction, her friends also helped her see the self-destructive patterns disrupting her flow.

They spoke out lies from my life and spoke truths into my life. I felt like they knew me better than I knew myself! I know that was God's voice speaking through them, because they saw things about me that were very much hidden within my soul.

In a raw and transparent community, blessings flow.

6.

The love and ministry shared by Maribel and Susan provided an example of Trinitarian flow.

Their relationship was not a simple association. They were more than acquaintances.

Real Trinitarian unity exists in collaboration, where you treat each other as you would your own family. It's a serving of one another, a preference for the other, and a respect for God's differing gifts.

This type of familial collaboration is fueled by the glory given to us, overspilling from the three-person Trinity. This gift of glory is an elevation, a supernatural position, a brightness that happens as we come together with others.

With Flow, relational love formed the core of our equipping strategy. Four different types of training helped catalyze Flow in community.

The Xealot Way Experience gave an overview of the cloud mindset and philosophy.

Flow Training provided assessment tools and Spirit discernment to help people discover their destiny through vision, history, and Scriptures.

Guide Training helped leaders integrate Flow into their organizations and relationships. Guides become like physical trainers but are holistic in their focus, walking with leaders day to day.

Sage Training is about teaching people how to mentor and influence others.

7.

For her birthday, Meg asked Maribel to take her to an amusement park.

At one and the same time, Maribel was:

Flattered to be asked.

Flattered because Meg was not the kind of girl who easily extended invitations.

And terrified, if the truth be told.

When they first met in one of the transition homes where Maribel volunteers, Meg was one of the young girls rescued from the slave trade.

On that Christmas day, Meg yelled at Maribel and handed back her gift.

You have no idea what my life is like!

When Maribel confessed that she, too, had found it difficult to work up much Christmas spirit, a conversation began.

Over time, Maribel and Meg shared stories of great suffering.

In the hopeful but still tentative relationship that developed, Meg risked an invitation.

Maribel was more than willing to battle her fear of heights if roller coasters were what her friend wanted on her birthday.

It just didn't help that the first ride was named Boomerang.

On the way up the hill, a white-knuckled Maribel confessed.

> *I told her how scared I was. I told her I was doing this in faith and only because of her.*

Descending, Maribel raised her hands like she did during praise.

> *That day, Meg opened up and I saw so many beautiful things about her. We dreamed of a future together, helping each other overcome our fears along the way.*

8.

In a cloud, dust and water vapor rise and are cooled in the higher atmosphere. Condensation occurs when water vapors return to their liquid state.

At that time, individual raindrops flow down together.

9.

In loving community, Maribel found her identity.

There is no greater gift than knowing who you are,
and they helped me understand that.

As a way to express her gratefulness, Maribel wrote a poem:

Star of the Sea

There was a lotus seed
drowning in a swamp of sorrow.

Full of dirt and living in complete darkness
in the stench of dead water.

But He had love, compassion, and mercy on the seed
and gave it strength to grow
and rise above the water
to see His light.

And so the seed bloomed with His fragrant love
to become a Star of the Sea,
which now lives in His living water.

Maribel discovered her name was from God.

Do you wish to rise?
Begin by descending.
You plan a tower that will pierce the clouds?
Lay first the foundation of humility.

— *Saint Augustine*

CHAPTER 7
LEADERSHIP IN THE CLOUD

1.

In the movie *X-Men*, Professor Xavier says it best:

> *A new generation of mutants is emerging, that much is certain. They will be called freaks, rebellious, mistakes, out of this world, crazy, and even genetic monstrosities.*

> *But they are emerging in farmlands, the inner cities, in the suburbs, in the deserts, and the jungles. And when they emerge, they will need teachers; people who can help them overcome their anger and show them how to use their strange gifts responsibly. They will need us.*

Left to themselves, mutants destroy themselves and others with their superpowers. Professor Xavier possessed a dangerous and brilliant plan.

He brought them into the academy to help them gain mastery of their inner selves and redirect their superpowers for good.

2.

For Jesus, the first step of leadership on this broken planet was down.

From heaven to earth.

From the pinnacle of praise to one familiar with suffering.

From omniscience to diapers.

From fellowship with God the Father to the thieves on a cross.

Ephesians tells us the end goal of equipping our people is so each person might become fully alive like Christ.

Like the blessing of rain, Jesus descended.

He became nothing; Philippians 2 shocks us.

Leadership in the cloud involves descending into greatness.

3.

As we picture clouds of people willing to radically, dangerously follow Jesus outside the walls of church, I imagine a people known for their:

Freedom.

Fearlessness.

Love.

Joy.

Collaborative spirit.

Humility.

Generosity.

Sacrificial giving.

Not just professional ministers, but Babel misfits of all types — artists, creatives, business persons, educators, politicians, students, and nonprofit leaders.

Ranging in age, but equally young at heart.

Not an association, but a group called to be a family.

Not a collection of individuals, but a shared story with names.

In the collection of clouds, I saw a flow of influence, moving in and out of assembly and blessing.

Together, in dangerous places, they experience:

> Discomfort and pain.
>
> Creativity and innovation.
>
> Robust experience.
>
> Supernatural change.
>
> Unspeakable joy.

4.

The leaders Jesus chose were not exactly who you might expect.

In the cloud, leaders should look out of kilter.

They live in the world more than in the church.

They don't fit a data trend, consumer index, or branding icon.

They are, in fact, misfits.

For equipping strategy, leaders:

> Focus on the small.
> Understand God causes the increase.
> Channel honor and yield credit.
> Pay attention to needs.
> Live to bless.
> Invest in others.
> Catalyze human development.
> Move with the flow.

They possess the same mindset of a parent who wants more for his or her own children.

5.

As Newsong continued to work to implement an equipping strategy as outlined in Ephesians 4, the concept of design moved front and center.

> The design of each person.

> The design of the body.

> The design of blessing.

Designs interwoven to form unity from diversity.

6.

The water cycle forms, transforms, and releases in God's design of blessing.

For each human, God weaves an intricate and intimate design of gift, passion, pain, personality, place, and experience.

The design, however, is never about making a name for oneself.

By collecting each unique, individual design, God forms a living mosaic of the local body — any place where at least two or three gather together in the name of Jesus.

God designed the one — each unique person — to vitally empower the other in an organic and supernatural work where the body flows outward in blessing.

7.

In Babel, the equipping manual comes with these chapters:

Shaping People to Help Carry the Load.

Inspiring People to Share the Vision.

Getting the Best People to Get the Job Done.

Babel fueled a necessary engine to release the power of the mass, while leaving people largely unseen and unknown.

Babel applies to more than just a focus on being big. It could be any other vision to make a name for the church:

Preaching the Gospel.

Reaching the lost.

Using the arts.

Finding yourself.

Name it Babel if a church:

Steers people away from being equipped for their unique destinies by resourcing them with technical products rather than a loving process.

As Newsong focused on lovingly releasing people into blessing, we customized our training.

The training involved accessing and releasing the emotional, intellectual, supernatural, and financial resources of each unique individual. The key to training was a customized assessment that determined their core competency levels in three areas:

Work.

Relationships.

Inner life.

This training was marked by:

Creativity.

Cultural immersions.

Learning through experience.

Individualized, well-coached plans.

Leveraging the power of the Spirit.

Our learning models became much more entrepreneurial, holistic, adaptive, systemic, and cross-cultural.

Rather than giving our people simple answers or a certain number of steps to follow, we began the dangerous work of equipping people not only with tools but, more importantly, with a way of generous living.

8.

With the hope of channeling superpowers to change the world, Professor Xavier brought the X-Men into the academy for training.

Did you notice? He doesn't hand any of them textbooks.

Instead, he entered into a relationship with each one.

Cloud leadership collects people together. As we trained our people for individual destinies, we did so in the design of community.

A critical role of Xealots leadership focused on strategically bringing people together in authentic, sacrificial community to eventually do kingdom work together.

In helping form critical relationships, we taught our people to:

Seek God for people with whom they can partner.

Unite with others who have the same heart and vision, but different gifts, cultural backgrounds, and networks.

Clarify expectations and potential goals.

Covenant among the group to equal commitment, passion, and sacrifice.

Affirm each other's gifts and destinies.

Weed out lies and misperceptions.

Share and enter into life stories, paying special attention to the thread of suffering.

Make time for one another by living life together.

Consider partners as family and serve each other with hearts of humility.

9.

A cloud teaches us:

Personal destinies are lived out collectively. Rain only falls in the process of vapors coming together. In the womb of a cloud, rain slowly forms.

To help us operate in the design of the body, Paul identified five core gifts of leadership in Ephesians 4:

> Apostle.
> Prophet.
> Evangelist.
> Teacher.
> Shepherd.

Operating in dynamic, living relationship, people exercise these differing gifts to form the core of leadership. Together, they become the servant-leadership team that inspires, trains, equips, and resources the cloud.

In diverse cultures, the meanings for each gift are shaped in different ways. I find it helpful to reframe this in the context of our own culture, in a way that I believe stays true to Paul's theology.

When I explain these five gifts to those outside the box of professional ministry, I often define them in the context of what I have found to be true in all healthy organizations. The gift is the same, but the name is different.

EPHESIANS TITLE	ALTERNATIVE TITLES	ROLES
Apostle	Visionary/ CEO	Catalyzes, lays foundations, entrepreneurial, touches all five key roles
Prophet	Voice/COO	Tells it like it is, the realist, sees the future and communicates it
Evangelist	Luminary/ Marketer	Inspires, leads others to the Light, winsome, socially warm, generates awareness and interest
Teacher	Sage/ Consultant/ Advisor	Creatively communicates truth, passes on critical life truths and rhythms
Shepherd	Father/ Human Resource Director/ Manager	Cares for and protects those being served

In addition to providing a synergy of perspectives and functions, the gifts operate together to form a critical balance.

Without the exercise of each gift:

> Apostles work out new ideas by using people.
>
> Prophets become belligerent or other-worldly.
>
> Evangelists neglect discipleship.
>
> Teachers fall into dogmatism or dry intellectualism.
>
> Shepherds value stability to the detriment of the mission.

In Ephesians 4, Paul writes that the purpose of equipping is:

> *To train Christ's followers in skilled servant work, working within Christ's body, the church, until we're all moving rhythmically and easily with each other, efficient and graceful in response to God's Son, fully mature adults, fully developed within and without, fully alive like Christ.*

10.

In building Babel, the vision is to grow bigger. The direction is up.

In a cloud, the purpose is to bless. The direction is down and out.

As we supernaturally bless, free, and equip people in the body, the focus naturally becomes to bless as we have been blessed.

In flow, they move out in the same fashion as the three persons of God, spilling love into the life of the other, over and over, into the very margins of His creation.

Only he shakes the heavens
and from its treasures takes out the winds.
He joins the waters and the clouds
and produces the rain.
He does all those things.
Only he realizes miracles permanently.

— Michael Servetus

CHAPTER 8

THROUGH THE CLOUDS

1.

Imagine with me:

A church like clouds freed to roam and bless the earth.

Freed from walls slowing the flow of love outward.

Freed from a vision focused on any singular agenda that detracts from a church's collective design to invest in their people.

Freed to flow with the Spirit, moving by the power and grace of a supernatural wind.

2.

Just before Phillip and Michelle Chang were to leave as missionaries to Korea, the company they built began to collapse.

Started in 2006 through the vision of Michelle and the execution of Phillip, the husband-and-wife team created Yogurtland, which grew into a chain of more than 300 stores in 20 states, with annual revenues of more than 200 million dollars.

Months before their scheduled departure for full-time ministry, the team responsible for leading the transition failed. The company was in a free fall, not in terms of value, but loss of values. The culture was like that of most other corporations — politics, power games, and pride.

Before the collapse, Phillip recalls:

> *I had an I-can-do-anything kind of mentality. Now, I was so scared, I suddenly felt I couldn't do anything. That was 100 percent God's grace that I lost confidence in myself.*

3.

Caught in the vortex of high school peer pressure, Karis found the spectacle of megachurch to be no match for alcohol-induced thrills in her community of friends.

Spiraling through a series of eating disorders and self-destructive behaviors, Karis was stopped one night at a police checkpoint and arrested for DUI.

Humiliated and broken, she told her father.

Her dad, a pastor, hugged her and said:

No matter what, we will always love you.

4.

Having helped develop the Staples Center, the StubHub Center, and the Kodak Theatre, David Lee worked with the movers and shakers — the Los Angeles Lakers and Clippers, a state governor, and numerous teams for the United States Tennis Association.

Talk about achieving the American dream for a child born in Hong Kong to Korean parents.

At the peak of his success, the stock market crash of 2008 left him with nothing. Millions of dollars, several real estate development projects, and even his own homes were replaced with frequent calls from creditors.

To make matters worse, a year later, during the week of Christmas, someone broke into a storage center that housed the last of the Lees' remains — wedding photos, furniture, favorite toys, bed sheets. Everything was stolen.

Living in a crowded home, through the generosity of

his sister, he was forced to cut short efforts to build a multiethnic church in Salt Lake City.

It was brutal, quite bloody, David recalls. *I was like one of the Israelites asking Moses if God had led them out of Egypt to kill them. How can God repay Godly endeavors in this way?*

The first round brought shock. The next brought clarity.

5.

Clouds are playful.

Imagine a church:

> Confident in destiny.
> Designed and equipped to bless.
> Understanding its role as conduit — not source
> — of blessing.

Flowing with the Spirit, we could:

> Shift.
> Twist.
> Stream.
> Transform.
> Float.
> Cascade.
> Tower.
> Roll.
> Thunder.

Mostly, I think we would Dance.

6.

With their dream of missionary work in Korea smashed, Phillip and Michelle Chang knew they needed to return to Yogurtland.

Broken down in confidence from the failure to develop a successful transition team, Phillip balked.

He told his wife and business partner that he no longer believed he could run the business.

Michelle replied:

> *Good. That's God's grace. You will have to depend on Him.*

7.

At some point after losing everything, David Lee began to stop asking:

Why?

Instead, he prayed:

What?

Change of perspective changed everything, David says. *God began to show me what renewed thinking was in the light of Romans 12:2.*

Don't copy the behavior and customs of this world, but let God transform you into a new person by changing the way you think. Then you will learn to know God's will for you, which is good and pleasing and perfect.

Lee understood that the way he thought about business had not spiritually matured into how a renewed mind thinks and sees.

Turning down many lucrative offers that may have restored his family's fortune, Lee felt led to start two new ventures — one focused on providing emergency food relief and another on prayer.

8.

Shortly after her arrest for DUI, Karis accepted her father's offer to send her to a ministry leadership group in Hawaii.

Karis wasn't thrilled about the idea. Church hadn't really worked for her, a pastor's child.

But Hawaii sounded cool.

On arrival, Karis made radical shifts in her understanding of the church:

Instead of going to events, she met these wild and free young people, a new generation of Jesus people.

Instead of programmed disconnection, she reveled in raw and caring relationships.

Instead of proper postures, she joined in David-like freedom in the sounds of worship.

9.

Clouds reflect beauty.

In changing light and different places, they display spectrums of:

Color.
Hue.
Texture.
Time.

Imagine our people displaying artistry well beyond the capability of any one self.

10.

Together, gifted as a husband-and-wife team, the Changs worked to restore Yogurtland back to their original values.

As they did so, they reminded their people of the company's roots.

A person in the Yogurtland family works to be:

> Totally honest.
> Totally kind.
> Creative.
> Passionate.
> A part of a team.

Through a renewed focus on training, the Changs reestablished a culture of honor, investing in each person for the sake of the other.

All of a sudden, their work began to feel like a full-time mission.

11.

In the prayer room he built for the community, David Lee experienced a vision from God.

It was a diagram of an incubator.

Included were sketches of a model to activate the 98 percent of people in church who will never enter full-time ministry, but who are equally called as CEOs, teachers, doctors, and marketplace leaders.

Having been gifted and experienced through God to do such work, David launched dcoEDGE in the spring of 2013.

His company has worked with hundreds of artists, entrepreneurs, businesses, churches, and nonprofits (including Xealots) for the community good.

12.

One day, in the middle of a youth celebration in Hawaii, God spoke to Karis:

> *I took you out of the muddy clay and placed you on a rock. I've given you a new song.*

A short time later, a young woman asked if she could pray over her. When she finished, unaware that God had spoken to Karis, the woman said:

> *I've got a vision for you.*
>
> *You had mud all over your body.*
>
> *God washed you completely clean.*
>
> *You stood up and began to sing.*

Later that same day, Karis phoned her father, who heard the story and cried tears of joy.

Wherever she travels in the world, Karis is especially in tune with those who suffer from addictions, identity crises, or family struggles.

God has taught her how to love people right where they are at.

13.

From an often merciless sun, clouds shade.

For those who:

Thirst,

suffer,

wander in oppressive heat...

the church is designed to provide relief and blessing.

14.

Through God's successful work to redeem their company, Phillip Chang gained a new perspective from an internal reality.

> *We didn't see our business as a full-time ministry. We were looking at it from an external perspective — measured by profits and performance. That's why we wanted to move to Korea to do "real" mission work. But what we have learned is that the change is internal.*

Looking at Yogurtland from a new perspective, they saw how God had designed them — individually and together — to be a blessing, small and large, for more than nearly 5,000 employees and millions of customers.

With renewed financial and spiritual health, the Changs envision continued growth, moving into the global marketplace.

At the same time, their focus has shifted to the one.

On a recent afternoon, while strolling through one of their stores, Phillip saw a little girl eating yogurt with her family.

In her smile, Phillip saw God's design from the start.

Their mission was for far greater profit.

15.

As the dcoEDGE leadership team develops version 2.0, which includes multimillion dollar portfolios, David Lee has learned to see God's hand in it all.

God led me on a journey to reboot the way I think about everything, including business and engaging the marketplace.

In his relationship with Xealots and Newsong, David found a community that believed, as he did, in the value of the marketplace believer and the power of suffering to shape the dreams God gives each one of us.

David recalls a story of sitting down with the producers of a film about a famous rapper. Having found favor as investors, one of the film's advisors, equally renown, sensed something different and commented that they preach excellence.

I sense something different with you guys. What kind of spirit is on you?

For David, it was confirmation that we are called to the dark places of the world; when we enter with the Light, people take notice.

We have permission to be dangerous with the Gospel.

16.

Following her return to faith, Karis experienced two powerful dreams.

In the one, she selected the most beautiful dress from a huge array of flowing gowns and wore it to dance on a spectacular ballroom floor inside a large white mansion.

In the other, many people ran away from a giant tsunami, while Karis and her friends, wearing sunglasses, turned and raced toward the wave, literally diving into its fury. On the other side of the wave, an old man swam in a pool on a large desert mountain. He invited Karis and her friends to swim with him.

Karis has often shared dreams with me.

I am her proud father, who loves to "swim" with her and her friends.

17.

The two dreams of Karis have come to represent a prophecy from the Prophet Joel:

> *I will pour out my Spirit*
> > *on every kind of people:*
> *Your sons will prophesy,*
> > *also your daughters.*
> *Your old men will dream,*
> > *your young men will see visions.*
> *I'll even pour out my Spirit on the servants,*
> > *men and women both.*
> *I'll set wonders in the sky above*
> > *and signs on the earth below.*

We are the bride, dancing with flowing white dresses in a sunlit grand ballroom. For each believer, it is an unsurpassed reality.

Freed from making a name for ourselves, we jump into the fury and danger of the world to glorify the name of Christ.

As Newsong continues the task of equipping more people to live out God's dream for their lives, I have come to believe each leap into the tsunami is well worth the risk.

18.

Clouds bless with rain, the source of life.

Imagine the church drenching scorched souls with living water.

19.

Have you experienced rain before it arrives?

You can smell it, feel it, hear it, almost taste it moving along a storm front.

In the midst of rethinking Newsong through the metaphor of the cloud, it's like that.

You sense a deluge coming.

The church as cloud:

> Flows with the winds of the Spirit, untamed and free.
>
> Resists brands, models, walls, prejudices, divides, and agendas.
>
> Defies the need for land, building, or other structure.
>
> Moves unconfined, uncontainable.
>
> Adapts to different cultures and communities.
>
> Sees, knows, and affirms each person and calls out each one's unique design and purpose.
>
> Equips each person with the mindset and tools to live out their personal destiny in a life-giving community.

It's the small cloud rising, no longer unseen, but an unstoppable force.

This is the supernatural rain that will soak us through and through, a baptism of resurrection.

Flow yields giving; giving liberates.

In Isaiah 58, the prophet writes:

> *Break the chains of injustice, get rid of exploitation in the workplace, free the oppressed, cancel debts. What I'm interested in seeing you do is: sharing your food with the hungry, inviting the homeless poor into your homes, putting clothes on the shivering ill-clad, being available to your own families. Do this and the lights will turn on, and your lives will turn around at once.*

Let the church pour out its people in blessing:

> Miracles will happen.
> The sick will be healed.
> The blind will see.
> Dreams and visions will be given.
> The dead will rise up.

From the fringes have come revolutions that changed the world:

> The American Revolution.
> The October Revolution.
> The Industrial Revolution.
> The Technological Revolution.

Now we're living in the midst of:

> A Spiritual Revolution.
> A Love Revolution.

People have been awakened to something more. They no longer want religion. They desire to see the real thing in human flesh, a power that cannot be held within the four walls of a church.

They seek a flow of love like water descending through clouds.

Let it rain!

Water is the driving force of all nature.

— Leonardo da Vinci

SUMMARY

Quick read, right? Hopefully, you're jumping up and down with joy knowing you're not crazy. There are some people like you who are sensing the same thing about the church and what it looks like now. You're part of this new vanguard of leaders known as the cloud!

So here's what we went over in this book, which is meant to inspire and provide language for what is happening to the church in today's shifts...

1.

The Four-Fold Purpose of the church (e.g. business, network, institution, small group, club, affinity group) as the cloud is to:

Roam Free.

Know.

Flow.

Bless.

2.

Freed from the Babel desire to rise through the clouds,
the church is freed to be the clouds.

To release a rain of blessing.

To be living water.

3.

ROAM FREE.

When I read Genesis 1 with new eyes, I got this image
of a cloud:

> *Be fruitful and multiply. Fill the earth and govern*
> *it. Reign over the fish in the sea, the birds in the sky,*
> *and all the animals that scurry along the ground.*

The purpose of humanity is to roam and bless the earth
to the very fringes of creation.

4.

KNOW.

In reimagining the church as a new metaphor, the water cycle teaches us about the critical nature of assembly.

In the same unstoppable flow of rivers moving to the sea, water evaporates, individual water vapors collect, and a small cloud rises.

Blessing remains impossible without coming together.

The woman at the well reveals a deep universal thirst to be known as God knows us.

John 4 tells us the woman dropped her bucket at the well and ran toward the village, telling everyone:

Come see a man who knows everything about me.

Individual drops of rain don't fall without first being formed in a collected community.

For the purpose of roaming and blessing the earth, the Body cannot function until we know each other.

Together in the context of a raw and loving community, we equip each other to help realize:

God's unique design for each person.

A new identity as a child of God.

An individual and collective destiny.

A shared purpose to bless.

5.

True knowledge erupts from a unity that is diverse.

Clouds form in a spectrum of surprising displays — all the way from light and whispery to dark and menacing.

In equipping our people for the purpose of blessing, we must see the beauty God sees in a design of diversity. No two clouds are identical.

Inside the walls of Babel, residents develop a love for the same jargon, dream, skin tone, culture, and creed.

To get beyond the walls of a church, our people must understand each one's unique design in the context of those different from them.

Clouds come with thousands of different names, shapes, and faces.

As we equip our people for blessing, the Body models diversity in power.

Our desire is not just to become *multi*ethnic, *multi*site, and *multi*cultural, but to be a church that flows and adapts. Comprised of ordinary people with superhuman powers, we become the living water. We are best when we are liquid and are shaped by the Spirit to demonstrate His love and presence.

In listing the five-fold gifts in Ephesians 4, Paul provides the church with tools to equip our people for blessing each other in a loving and highly diverse assembly.

6.

FLOW.

Jesus in John 5: He does only what he sees the Father
doing.

Self-giving for the glory of the other.

The same flow moves Jesus on his walk to Calvary, his
life spilling out in love for us.

The same flow moves us to see our blessing as glory to
God.

7.

BLESS.

In a collection of clouds, a water droplet forms when the climate cools and vapors condense.

Driven by the wind, tiny drops of water release life-giving blessing to the ends of the earth.

When clouds dance, you see hints of an unstoppable flow moving out of a supernatural Trinity.

EPILOGUE

As I write, Newsong has just formally launched a new season of doing church as defined by the metaphor of the cloud. Since returning from Thailand with a new vision for the church, it has been a 10-year journey down an often arduous path. I wouldn't trade a day of it!

We have transitioned from being a typical suburban church to what is now a more diverse and urban church. The city we are now in is mostly Hispanic and Asian. It is more culturally and economically diverse.

I do not intend to denigrate suburban churches at all. We need them. Suburban churches are filled with middle class, homogenous, young people who hunger for adventure and wildness that can best be found in Jesus. At the same time, many homogenous churches that fill the landscape of our countries are primarily program- and comfort- driven.

The shift for me is being Spirit-driven, which often leads us down a road of pain and pruning.

I am learning this: We can have joy, but it gets ugly.

The biggest shift I noticed is how our move brought us back to the heart of our original vision and values. Over time, even our more progressive church attracted settlers who didn't necessarily come because of our vision. The move actually brought our true, core Newsong family together...folks who came because of our mission. It was a gift to us, and it released those who had another direction in mind.

Clouds often bring blessings through storms. With deluges come flooding. Lightning sets fires. Tornadoes and hurricanes and cyclones destroy. Danger and discomfort are sometimes part of the process of producing life-giving rain.

I have also realized that there are haters. Sure, we all screw up and make mistakes, but there are people who will never let it go. In fact, they knowingly or unknowingly are toxic to others. So expect criticism and complainers. Amazing brings hazing.

But in the end, it's worth it! You could feel the new air, freedom, and joy as we turned our church around to focus on being a HOME where we love and an ACADEMY where we equip people to flourish outside our walls.

THE CLOUD MANIFESTO

We are a community of misfits,
who zealously love God
and the misfits of the world,
even in the midst of suffering and pain.

We believe in the Primacy of Love.
We believe Justice is the hard work of love
and that the test of our maturity
is our love for the outsider.

We possess the ability to flow like a cloud,
to be shapeless and formless,
a force you cannot stop.
We never become more like God
than when we lovingly adapt to others not like us.

We desire unity over conformity,
and diversity, miracles, and beauty
through conversations and presence.
It's about the walk, not just the talk.

We believe great relationships birth great visions.

We collaborate by bringing together
different gifts and equal sacrifice,
bonded in love like a healthy family.

We believe that the church cannot be contained
on a piece of land, so we live free to roam the whole earth.

We are called to bless the earth —
that is, to see, know, affirm, and
give away generously of ourselves.

Our mission is to roam and bless,
unleashing the beauty and love of God to all the nations.

We believe movements start
from the margins with the misfits,
both the resourced and under-resourced.

We believe in the supernatural work of the Spirit.
We are fueled by Him.
We are guided by Him.
We love because He first loved us.

We carry in us Love, Joy, Freedom, Hope, Peace, and
An Extraordinary Spirit.

We are God's hands, heart, and feet in everything we do.

WHAT'S NEXT?

Practical Design Principles in forming clouds where you are:

Whether you're an institutional church, a business, a group of creatives, a network, a house church, or a life group, the small cloud rises in the context of blessing, knowing, and flowing.

I'd love to share a simple blueprint that God has unfolded for us as we've worked with churches, networks, and organic movements globally. My guess is that many of the cross-cultural, third-culture principles apply to what you hope to do:

http://www.smallcloudrising.com

There you will find ideas for moving forward, which should be centered around these understandings...

REDEFINE CHURCH.

It's not a building. It's a group of people called out to love God and love people, especially the misfits. We renamed each one of our church buildings. Instead of naming our buildings Newsong, they are called 10TEN or theHUB. This reflects our belief that the building is not the church, but simply one of the places where the church meets.

PURPOSES.

A cloud roams free to know, flow, and bless.

LEADERSHIP.

The leadership composition of a cloud is the five-fold gifts: Apostle, Prophet, Evangelist, Teacher, and Shepherd.

VALUES.

The key values are Love, Equip, and Unity. Learn to design structures around loving and equipping. Training needs to focus on helping people flourish outside the church. The church often traps people into service inside its walls.

WHAT IF?

What if you love the idea and image of a church as a cloud, but you have the mindset of Babel, focused on building up and not moving out?

Here are a few design principles to consider:

THINK HYBRID.

When new technologies are developed, sometimes general acceptance happens with mixtures. If the electric car was first introduced before the hybrid electric and gas, it probably wouldn't have been accepted as readily. Hybrids are common in the midst of transition.

CREATE A TEAM OF LEADERS FOCUSED ON INNOVATION.

Give the team great opportunities to explore, question, and take risks with models. The discoveries from this team will affect your core constituency over time.

LAUNCH NEW MODELS DIFFERENT FROM WHAT YOU'RE USED TO.

Business leaders do it all the time. They know that for their company to grow and flourish, they need to diversify to handle economic and cultural shifts. Don't put all your eggs in one basket!

COLLABORATE.

We don't always have to launch new models of church ourselves, but we can partner with those who do. One of the tests of my collaboration maturity is a willingness to not take the credit! We need to live and give generously to those God has tasked with different and creative missions, instead of just focusing on our own.

This is a dynamic book, as the church is alive and growing! To continue on the journey, stay connected to us.

http://www.facebook.com/smallcloudrising

http://www.smallcloudrising.com

http://www.facebook.com/davegibbons

http://www.oneloveus.org

http://www.newsong.net

http://www.xealots.org

http://www.dcoedge.com

ANNOTATIONS

_____

_____

_____

_____

_____

_____

_____

_____

_____

_____

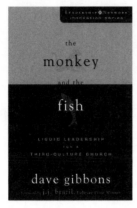

THE MONKEY AND THE FISH
Liquid leadership for a third-culture church

Our world is marked by unprecedented degrees of multiculturalism, ethnic diversity, social shifts, international collaboration, and technology-driven changes. The changes are profound, especially when you consider the unchecked decline in the influence, size, and social standing of the church. There is an undercurrent of anxiety in the evangelical world, and a hunger for something new. And we're sensing the urgency of it. We need fresh, creative counterintuitive ways of doing ministry and church and leading it in the 21st century. We need to adapt. Fast.

XEALOTS
Defying the gravity of normality

What does Jesus mean when he promises "life to the full"? Like many Christians, author Dave Gibbons thought "life to the full" meant just the positives – a life full of joy and happiness. After all, isn't that what we're taught in seminars, in self-help books, and even in psychological assessments to ascertain who is – and is not – a "good fit"? We look for people with lots of successes and strengths, don't we? Gibbons' own beliefs on the subject were rocked when he took a long, hard, honest look at his own life and realized it was his failures that made him who is today.